CLIMBING

OUTDOOR ADVENTURES

DAVID ARMENTROUT

The Rourke Press, Inc.
Vero Beach, Florida 32964

David Armentrout specializes in nonfiction writing and has had several book series published for primary schools. He resides in Cincinnati with his wife and two children.

PHOTO CREDITS
© Gordon Wiltsie: cover, pages 10, 16, 18; ©East Coast Studios: pages 6, 13, 15, 19, 21, 22; © Corel Corporation: pages 4, 7, 12; © Wayne Aldridge/International Stock: page 9

EDITORIAL SERVICES:
Penworthy Learning Systems

Library of Congress Cataloging-in-Publication Data

Armentrout, David, 1962-
    Climbing / David Armentrout.
        p. cm. — (Outdoor adventures)
    Includes bibliographical references (p.24) and index.
    Summary: Examines the different kinds of climbing, on mountains, rocks, and ice, and discusses techniques, how to learn, safety aspects, and competitions.
    ISBN 1-57103-203-7
    1. Mountaineering—Juvenile literature. [1. Mountaineering.] I. Title II. Series:
Armentrout, David. 1962- Outdoor adventures.
GV200.A757 1998
796.52'2—dc21   98–18419
                                                                                    CIP
                                                                                    AC

Printed in the USA

TABLE OF CONTENTS

A CHALLENGING SPORT

People have been climbing mountains for centuries. Early explorers climbed mountains to map new lands. Native Americans climbed mountains to spot herds of buffalo—their main source of food and clothing.

Today many people climb mountains because climbing is fun and challenging. Mountain climbing can also be hard work for the body and mind.

A safety rope, crampons, and a backpack are some of the things you will use when climbing.

MOUNTAIN CLIMBING

Most people think of climbers dressed from head to toe in special clothing, while climbing a snow-capped mountain. This is one form of mountain climbing, but there are others.

Making your way down a mountain is just as hard as going up.

When climbing, make sure you do not grab or step on a loose rock.

Rock climbing and ice climbing are two other forms of mountain climbing. They both require the use of special climbing gear.

Some climbers do not use any gear. They use only their hands and feet to climb. This kind of climbing is called scrambling, and it is the simplest form of the sport.

CLIMBING TO THE TOP

Some climbers set goals to reach the top of the world's highest mountains. The tallest mountains are in Southeast Asia. Mount Everest is the tallest at 29,028 feet (8847.7 meters) above sea level. Many people have reached the top, and many lives have been lost trying. It is a long, hard climb.

Many challenging, but smaller, mountains have been climbed in North America. Alaska's Mount McKinley and Washington's Mount Rainier are both in national parks and draw many visitors and climbers.

You would need a lot of experience to climb this big mountain.

ROCK CLIMBING

The goal in rock climbing is the same as in mountain climbing—to reach the top. Rock climbers practice on small hills and cliffs, not on mountains like Alaska's Mount McKinley.

Rock climbing is done on a rock **face** (FAYS), or wall. Climbers place their hands and feet in **holds** (HOLDZ) as they make their way up the wall. Holds are small openings, cracks, and ledges.

Climbers use ropes and clips, which protect them if they should lose their grip and fall. A climbing buddy, called a **belayer** (bi LAY er), holds the rope tight as the climber moves up the wall.

Practice climbing on boulders that are close to the ground.

ICE CLIMBING

Climbing ice is like climbing rock. You climb straight up with a goal to reach the top.

Ice climbers need more gear than rock climbers. They carry one or two ice axes that they use to cut steps and holds into the ice wall.

Ice climbers can use an ax to hold, or **belay** (bi LAY), the rope.

Special gear like ice axes and crampons are used to grip the ice.

Climbers carry crampons in their backpacks then stop to put them on when needed.

The rope is called dry rope and is made to use in wet places.

Ice climbers also wear **crampons** (KRAM pahnz). Crampons are metal spikes that fasten to climbing boots. With crampons on their boots, climbers can walk and climb on packed snow and ice without slipping.

RAPPELLING

Climbers who go up must come down. **Rappelling** (ra PEL ling) is one way to get down a steep cliff.

A climber hammers a U-shaped metal **anchor** (ANG kur) into the rock at the top of the cliff. A rope is threaded through the anchor, and the climber uses the rope to rappel down the cliff. Climbers can wear a harness or hold rope around their waists.

A climber rappels by pushing off the cliff's face and letting out some rope at the same time. Many climbers enjoy the thrill of backing over the side of a cliff and sliding down a rope to the bottom.

When rappelling, make sure you have a buddy to hold a safety rope.

LEARNING TO CLIMB

Climbing is a fun, exciting sport. People young and old are trying it for the first time. It is important to have your body in good shape. Daily exercise and stretching muscles before a climb make climbing easier.

There are skills that you must learn before climbing. An instructor will teach you about climbing gear and the basic climbing skills. A climbing instructor will also show you how to pick the best route up a mountain and what to do if an accident or injury occurs.

Beginners become good climbers by practicing and testing their skills.

Learning the right way to climb from an instructor is important.

CLIMBING SAFELY

Climbing can be a risky sport. Even good climbers can make mistakes and injure themselves. For the safest climb, make sure your gear is in good shape. Always wear a helmet and the proper clothing.

Proper climbing shoes help your feet grip the rock.

Climbing rope should be checked for safety before every climb.

Climbing should never be done alone. Climbing works best as a team sport. A climbing buddy helps you with your ropes and can stop you if you fall.

People who climb big mountains climb in teams. A team might have 10 or more climbers, all with different skills. Team members help each other.

CLIMBING CONTESTS

As climbing has become more popular, so have climbing contests. Climbing contests are held all over the world, but you don't have to travel to the mountains to compete. Most large cities have indoor climbing walls.

One popular contest is wall climbing. Two climbers race up a natural or man-made wall, and the first to reach the top wins. Climbers of all ages enjoy testing their own skill level as well as testing themselves against other climbers.

A climbing wall is a great way to start climbing.

GLOSSARY

anchor (ANG kur) — an object used to hold other objects in place

belay (bi LAY) — to wind or wrap a rope to hold it or stop it from moving

belayer (bi LAY er) — a climbing partner who keeps the climbing ropes from moving

crampons (KRAM pahnz) — metal spike attachments for climbing boots that keep a climber's feet from slipping; climbing irons

face (FAYS) — the front, or wall, of a cliff or mountain

holds (HOLDZ) — places in rocks, such as cracks and ledges, to put hands and feet for climbing

rappelling (ra PEL ling) — to come down from a cliff or mountainside by means of a belayed rope that is let out smoothly a few feet at a time

This climber stands high on a mountain glacier.

INDEX

FURTHER READING

Find out more about Outdoor Adventures with these helpful books:
Lund, Bill. *Rock Climbing.* Capstone Press, 1996.
Brimner, Larry Dane. *Rock Climbing.* Watts, 1997.